COJOURN

Companion Guide and Workbook

Molly Keehn, Ed.D. and **Karl Henricksen**

CoJourn
STAY THE PATH WITH "TOGETHER-HELP"

Book cover design by Charlyn Samson
Original cover art by Pablo Iranzo Duque
Caricature art by Nick Sullivan
Authors photograph by Amanda Herman

ISBN Paperback: 978-1-7340200-2-1
ISBN Ebook: 978-1-7340200-3-8
Printed in the United States of America
First Printing, 2020

CONTENTS

WELCOME

Welcome to the CoJourn Companion Guide and Workbook!

This resource is recommended to use alongside our book, *CoJourn: Harnessing the Power of Connection to Tune into Your Wisdom, Achieve Your Goals, and Create the Life You Want,* or to support your learning after attending a CoJourn workshop / training, or as part of an organizational program. It is not intended to replace any of these more comprehensive ways to learn about CoJourn.

As you embark on your journey through CoJourn, it can be helpful to have a quick and accessible reference to remind you about the various aspects of the program. The guide includes summaries of key concepts and activities that are designed to support what you learned and walk you through each step of the process of your CoJourn experience. It also includes some questions for reflection, and other activities that will be helpful to talk through with your CoJourn Partner. Ultimately, similar to the Quick Start Guide to a car (in contrast to the comprehensive Owner's Manual), we hope it will serve as a handy reference when you are in the midst of the process of CoJourn.

As you move through learning and applying CoJourn, we want to remind you that this program is meant to benefit *YOU* and to be something that brings you more connection, support, and motivation to follow-through on your goals. The program is based on research-backed strategies that have worked for thousands of CoJourn participants world-wide. We recommend that you follow the core principles of the program, even if they may feel new or uncomfortable. However, it is also important to remember that we are all different. So, if after trying them out, if any parts are not working for you and your partner, we encourage you to adapt and make it work for your individual circumstances and needs. Only you are the expert on your own experience!

We would love to hear from you as you move through CoJourn. You can email us at connect@cojourn.org or connect with us through our social media pages, @cojourninternational (Instagram) and https://www.facebook.com/cojourn (Facebook).

Remember to experiment, and be curious and compassionate with yourself and your partner as you move through CoJourn.

And don't forget, the magic of possibility is always in the air. Whatever change you need, big or small, there's no time like the present!

Molly and Karl, CoJourn Cofounders

OVERVIEW

What is CoJourn?

CoJourn is a personal growth and goal achievement program that trains pairs of people to partner up for more external accountability, connection, and support as they go after their goals and dreams. The program helps you prioritize what matters most to you while connecting with a partner you choose for mutual support and accountability.

The program's mission is to:

1. Counter the increased disconnection we experience in our fast-paced, technology-driven society, and
2. Provide an accessible tool to help with follow-through on a single life intention over time (the program is designed for the length of either 12 weeks, or one year).

CoJourn

Authentic Connection

Sustainable Follow-Through

How Does it Work?

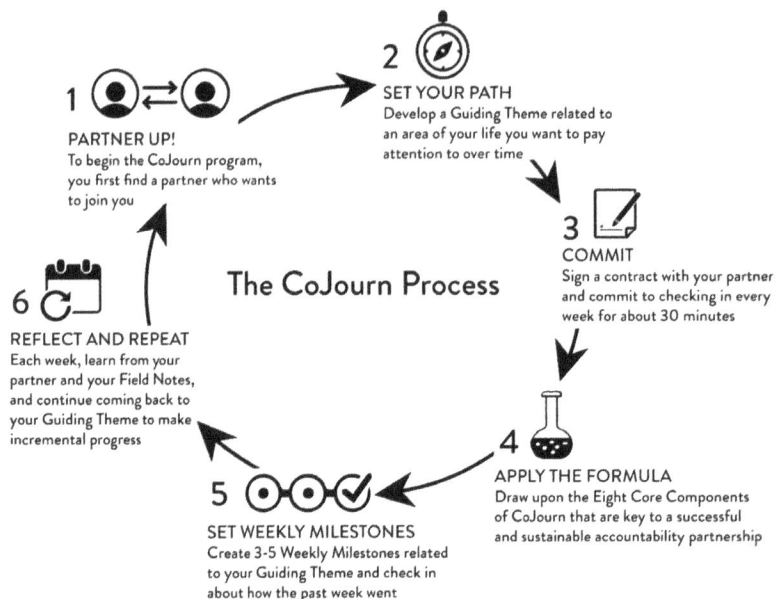

The CoJourn Process

1 **PARTNER UP!**
To begin the CoJourn program, you first find a partner who wants to join you

2 **SET YOUR PATH**
Develop a Guiding Theme related to an area of your life you want to pay attention to over time

3 **COMMIT**
Sign a contract with your partner and commit to checking in every week for about 30 minutes

4 **APPLY THE FORMULA**
Draw upon the Eight Core Components of CoJourn that are key to a successful and sustainable accountability partnership

5 **SET WEEKLY MILESTONES**
Create 3-5 Weekly Milestones related to your Guiding Theme and check in about how the past week went

6 **REFLECT AND REPEAT**
Each week, learn from your partner and your Field Notes, and continue coming back to your Guiding Theme to make incremental progress

To Be Successful with CoJourn, Follow These 8 Simple Steps!

STEP 1: Find a partner

STEP 2: Learn about the 8 Core Components of CoJourn with your partner

STEP 3: Commit

STEP 4: Develop a Guiding Theme

STEP 5: Create and Record Weekly Milestones to make progress with your Guiding Theme

STEP 6: Meet Weekly with Partner for 30 minutes to offer mutual support, check-in on progress and set new milestones for the upcoming week

STEP 7: Work with Your Partner and Make Adjustments Along the Way

STEP 8: Reflect along the way, and **Celebrate** the small wins to create success-minded forward momentum and a program that works for *you*

STEP 1

Find a Partner for CoJourn

My partner served as an unshakeable mirror who created the opportunity for me to introspect, gain self-awareness, and instill corrective action where needed.

– Michael Funk, Ed.D., paired with a friend

The premise of CoJourn is that the program is done with someone else. We encourage you to think carefully about people in your life who you could work with for this adventure.

Only you can decide who might work best for you. Below are some tips to give you a hand.

First, make a list of potential partners:

Start by looking at the people around you. CoJourn is a fantastic way to get to know someone new, or a great way to have more regular contact with a person you have known for a long time. Think outside of the box—the key criteria are that it is a person you think you can trust, and who would be interested in doing it.

Ideally, Your Partner Should . . .

- **Be somebody you trust:** The whole program rests on being able to open up to your CoJourn partner (even the slightest bit) about what is going on in your life. Everything said during program check-ins is confidential, so you want to pick somebody who you believe can keep what you share to themselves and someone you would feel at least somewhat comfortable opening up to. In the beginning, most teams have more surface level check-ins, but over time, you may be surprised by how much you each begin to feel comfortable sharing with your partner.

- **Be someone you like:** You don't necessarily need to know your CoJourn partner well, but it should be somebody you would enjoy talking with and would like to continue to get to know better. It's not a good idea to pair with someone who triggers you or with whom you have an especially rocky history. Ideally, this person should be someone you would look forward to talking with for a half-hour each week.
- **Be somebody who will follow through:** Because CoJourn entails a commitment to meet weekly, it is a good idea to think about that as you choose your partner. Does this person have a history of agreeing to things and then flaking out? Will it be possible for them to schedule a half-hour meeting every week? Even if there are doubts, it's not necessarily a deal breaker; often, a pre-program chat about expectations and concerns can help immensely.
- **Have similar availability to talk on the phone or in person:** Usually teams can find a time to talk during the week that can work for both people without too much of a problem (commute time and/or lunch breaks can be great ways to sneak in check-ins). However, this is important to think about as you choose your partner. Is this person in the same time zone as you? If not, will you be able to work with that? Do you have any overlaps in free time during the week or on the weekends?

Ideally, Your Partner Should Not . . .

- **Be someone you want to change or fix:** It is very important that this program be about making change for yourself while getting support from and supporting someone else in their own process of change. However, it does not work if you go in with a preset idea of *how* you want your partner to change. That is for them to decide.
- **Be someone you are intimidated by or put on a pedestal:** CoJourn is based in a kind, nonjudgmental approach to change. And so, you want your partner to be someone you feel comfortable showing your imperfections to. If you are intimidated by someone, have a pattern of comparing yourself to them, or feel that they have it all together so maybe they can help you, that probably won't be the best match. (Though, if you did partner with them, perhaps you would get to see firsthand that they, too, have their own insecurities and imperfections).
- **Be someone you have a crush on:** CoJourn can create an intimate relationship with someone, and you will have someone you can really show yourself to. At times this deep, intimate relationship may get confusing, particularly if your CoJourn partner is someone you are physically attracted to. Though it is possible to work through this, we advise choosing a partner for whom this would not be a problem from the start. (Then you can make goals so you can get enough courage to ask that person you DO have a crush on, out on a date!)

- **Be someone who wants to work on something that would be painful or triggering for you:** As you approach potential partners, you will want to make sure that you feel comfortable with their Guiding Theme and are able to support them with it. For example, if you have a history of struggling with an eating disorder, it may be difficult to be paired with someone who wants to focus on diet and exercise.

Examples of Potential CoJourn Pairings:

Parent/Child — Siblings — College roommates (current or past)
Friends — Bandmates Colleagues — Grandparent/Grandchild
Teammates — Members of Professional Organizations

We believe that with intentionality and support any pairing could work for this program. However, we offer these guidelines as a way to avoid some of the common pitfalls.

Tips to ask someone to be your CoJourn Partner

For some, asking someone to be your CoJourn partner can feel nerve-wracking. This is a common feeling, but the truth is that most people are extremely honored to be invited to be someone's partner, regardless of whether or not they are up for it. This type of personal growth program is not for everyone.

It is helpful to be patient and to find someone who really wants to try the program with you. Along with inviting people individually, another way to look for a partner is to post on social media, or send an email to a group or listserv. CoJourn can be tricky to explain, so sending them a little information (or a copy of our book!) can be a helpful way to initiate this conversation.

Below are a couple of emails you could adapt:

Email #1 (Mad Libs style)

Dear [potential amazing CoJourn partner],

I recently learned about a really [adjective that works for you!] program that sounds like something I'd like to try. It is called CoJourn, and it's a goal-setting and peer-support program that helps you to go after longer-term goals and intentions with a partner.

The whole premise of the program is that having someone to be accountable to can help with follow-through. It involves setting a long-term Guiding Theme and using the program's structure to check in (over the phone or in person) with a self-selected partner every week about progress. The time commitment is thirty minutes a week over the course of the program (typically 12 weeks, or a year).

As I was brainstorming potential partners to invite to try it out with me, you were the first person I thought of. It would be so [adjective] to get the chance to talk to you once a week, and I think we could have a lot of fun supporting each other on our goals.

You can read more about the program here: www.cojourn.org.

Let me know what you think!

And, if it feels like too much for you right now, I completely understand—but I wanted to make sure that I asked.

Email #2 (written by a current CoJourn participant)

Dear _____,

I'm about to launch into a few professional projects simultaneously, which is exciting and a bit daunting. I also have some [personal health goals]. Therefore, I'm seeking an accountability partner for the next six months or so. Might that be you?

Together we would:

- set goals (personal or professional).
- talk on the phone weekly for thirty minutes (fifteen minutes each), to check in and share about progress on our individual goals and offer support / insights if requested by a partner.

If you're reading this and feel a sense of excitement and maybe relief, then let's talk! If instead it feels like "just another thing to do," then probably it's not right for you.

Are you interested? Let me know by [Friday 2/16] please.

Partner Matching

Some participants in CoJourn programs within organizations, or as part of our cohort program, may choose to be matched with a CoJourn partner. This can be a wonderful way to meet someone new, and build another relationship. When pairing partners, we ask a series of questions about your goals, significant identities, geographical location, and time availability for check-in meetings. Since CoJourn centers peer support, rather than coaching, any partnership should work. However, we do our best to accommodate requests with regards to preferences (this depends on the size of the pool of participants, of course). For example, a participant may prefer to work with another woman, someone in their age group, or someone in their geographical time zone.

STEP 2

Learn about the 8 Core Components— The CoJourn Formula for Success

CoJourn is based on 8 Core Components—the research-backed strategies that are so essential for success with the program. This is what distinguishes CoJourn from other accountability programs.

Some of these guidelines may seem like no-brainers, and others may feel like a very different way from how you typically do things. We encourage you to use these as guideposts to structure your experience, to refresh your memory on them throughout the process, and to check in with your partner about how you feel you are doing with them.

1) Peer Support
2) Confidentiality
3) Active Listening
4) Accountability
5) Commitment
6) Compassionate / Nonjudgmental Approach
7) Spirit of Celebration
8) Singular Focus on Change

The first three Core Components above relate to cultivating connection with your CoJourn Partner. Following these component guidelines will support the creation of a trusting, sustainable, and vibrant relationship with your partner, and help keep potential tangles or challenging dynamics to a minimum.

The final five components of the program all relate to creating conditions to maximize follow-through, helping participants to make real, sustained movement toward their goals.

Component #I: Peer Support

We support each other, without letting each other off the hook (a subtle distinction).
    – Sandy, 67, CoJourn participant, partnered with college roommate

In contrast to models of peer coaching or peer mentoring, CoJourn is a model of Peer Support that taps into the power of reciprocity and mutuality.

Peer Support Involves:

- Holding an open space and listening compassionately to your partner so they can access their own wisdom about what is right for them, and most needed at that moment in time,
- Acting as a non-judgmental sounding board and encouraging your partner, striving to be positive and supportive of what they are going through,
- Reminding your partner of their Guiding Theme each week before they start setting their Weekly Milestones,
- Asking clarifying questions to help your partner distill the 3-5 most important goals to strive toward that week,
- Recording your partner's goals for them, using a clear and encouraging tone.

Peer Support Does Not Involve:

- Offering unsolicited feedback,
- Coaching / advising your partner about what you think their goals should be,
- Asking questions in a way that indicates disapproval or judgment about their goals, (i.e., "Do you really think you should do that?"),
- Shifting the focus to you while your partner is talking, (i.e., "Oh yeah, that reminds me of that time when I . . .").

More Tips for Peer Support

What happens when I have a good idea to share?
At times you may have a really good idea or advice you would like to offer your CoJourn partner. This is great! But it is important to always ask permission first, to see if they want to hear it (e.g., "I have an idea about how you might navigate that situation and a goal that might help support you with it. Are you interested in hearing it?"). As a general

policy, always avoid unsolicited feedback and trust that we each usually hold the wisdom we need inside of us.

What if I want some coaching?
It is always okay to ask for your partner's help or advice if you find you are having trouble developing your goals. This can be particularly helpful during times of struggle. Plus, your partner may have a useful perspective based on your patterns and goals from the past. The key is to make this the exception, rather than the rule, and work on trusting your own innate wisdom about what might be best for you.

How do I work with pre-existing relationship patterns?
Engaging in Peer Support may be particularly challenging in relationships that already have a coaching dynamic in place (e.g. parent/child, siblings, or romantic partners), so it is essential to pay close attention to this component, and check in regularly with your partner. Regular process check-ins can help (see instructions and guided questions later in this guidebook).

Component #2: Confidentiality

If you didn't have that air of confidentiality, and that promise of confidentiality, the program would never get to the level that it gets to. It's really important. So, it's good. It's really good. And it's challenging.
— Betty, 65, CoJourn Participant, paired with her daughter

It is critical that both CoJourn partners feel assured that everything said within the confines of a CoJourn check-in will be confidential (not be repeated without permission).

- This helps CoJourn partners to feel comfortable and as if they can show themselves to one another and be vulnerable.
- Similar to therapeutic relationships, this helps create a safe place to talk. With the rise of social media and confusing boundaries between public and private spaces, these spaces of confidentiality are even more rare and coveted.

Tips for Honoring Confidentiality

Discuss It

Be sure to have a conversation with your partner about what confidentiality means to them. Some people may want the fact that they are participating in CoJourn to be totally confidential. Others may be open to sharing that they are involved with the program, while just having the contents of the check-ins confidential.

A Caution

Be particularly careful when you have dual / overlapping relationships with your CoJourn partner (i.e., if you are a parent, doing the program with your child, be careful that you don't share any information that was said in a check-in with your spouse or co-parent.)

An Exception

If you feel concerned that your partner is experiencing a mental health crisis and is in danger of hurting themselves or others, it is important to break confidentiality and get in touch with some outside help. If you are doing the program on your own, you could express your concern to another member of their family or one of their friends without sharing details of their CoJourn check-in. If you are part of an organizational program, you can contact the liaison within the organization who is coordinating CoJourn, or a CoJourn coach within the organization. There are also national hotlines you can call for support and advice from professionals. In the U.S. you can contact the National Suicide Prevention Lifeline at 1-800-273-8255, the National Alliance of Mental Illness hotline at 1-800-950-6264 or helpline@nami.org or you can text the Crisis Text Line by texting "HOME" to 741741.

Component #3: Active Listening

Having each other's support was so critical because there was some thinking in my own head that I needed to get out. I hadn't before had an outlet for it where I had what felt like a loving, caring hug on the other end of the line listening to me, and thinking I was the bomb no matter what I did. I think it helped me process and work through my own insecurities and my own challenges that I probably wouldn't have done.
      – Ingrid, 34, CoJourn participant paired with her cousin

Active listening, at the most basic level, is hearing and receiving a message with understanding.

CoJourn check-ins are rooted in this intentional type of listening practice that involves striving to listen with your full, undivided presence and attention.

- This type of active, deep listening relates closely to peer support, and helps CoJourn partners act as sounding boards, and pull out each other's thinking about what they need.
- None of us get enough opportunities to be truly listened to, and it's a real gift we can offer one another.

Tips for Active Listening During the Check-In

- **Take a few deep breaths** beforehand to center yourself and set an intention to listen with your full, undivided attention.
- **Minimize distractions** by moving to a space in which you can be fully present.
- **Avoid multitasking** during check-ins (stay off of email, Facebook, etc.).
- **Listen without judging** or reacting until the full message is shared.
- **Be compassionate with yourself** if your mind wanders, but gently bring your mind back to what your partner is saying.
- **Record your partner's goals** for them as they talk – this supports active involvement in listening to your partner.

Component #4: Accountability

Having to be accountable to someone really does change your behavior, in a way that being accountable just to myself doesn't. For me, I am really good at letting myself off the hook. I think that having just told one other person, 'I'm going to try to do these three things this week,' makes it possible.

— Gloria, 37, CoJourn participant paired with her mother

CoJourn is based on belief in the value of external accountability to help people close the gap between intention and action and follow through on life goals. One of the reasons New Year's resolutions are so difficult to follow-through on is that there is often no one to offer support or hold you accountable over time.

Definition

Merriam-Webster's dictionary defines accountability as "an obligation or willingness to accept responsibility or to account for one's actions." In the context of CoJourn, this means simply telling someone that you are planning to do something, writing it down, and then following up and reporting on how it went.

Research Shows

The simple act of writing a goal down, sharing it with a friend, and checking in weekly about it, makes people 76% likely to actually achieve it (33% more likely than people who did not build in that type of accountability).[1]

Legitimate Accountability

The form of accountability in CoJourn is what is called, "legitimate accountability." This means being accountable to someone or something that you actually want to be accountable to, in relation to something that you believe in and have bought into. In most cases, for accountability to be truly effective as a strategy, it must be perceived as legitimate (i.e., a chosen accountability partner).[2]

When participating in CoJourn, you get to select your own partner—someone you trust and hold in high regard, so this creates a powerful form of "legitimate" accountability that can aid in changing habits and going after what you want.

Component #5: Commitment

I think [the program works so well] partly because it's a commitment. It's not "seven days to get this thing done" or "twenty-one days to change a habit." So you really need to just make peace with whatever is in the way for you to be accountable. So, for me, the length of the program is so big in a way . . . there's no sense in sort of weaseling your way out, or letting yourself off the hook. It's like, you're here, you're staying. Figure something out.

— Samantha, 38, CoJourn Participant paired with her mother

CoJourn involves making a dual commitment—both to yourself AND another person. This increases the likelihood of following through on the program.

30 Minutes a Week

You commit to give yourself the gift of 30 minutes a week, to slow down and check in to make sure you are going in the direction you set for yourself. Commitment to this mechanism for consistent self-reflection provides a rich opportunity to practice mindfulness in today's fast paced society.

Full Program Commitment

You commit to connecting with your partner on the phone or in person every week at a consistent time over the course of the program (12 weeks or a year). While it may be easy to let yourself off the hook, it is more difficult to skip out on a check-in when you know that there is someone else who is counting on it for their own well-being.

Tips for Sustaining the Commitment

Keep a Consistent Time

We encourage teams to develop a consistent weekly time to meet (e.g., every Wednesday at 5:00 pm). That way, participants can structure their life around their check-ins, almost as if they would plan around a staff meeting at work. This can save a lot of energy and reduce the exasperation of trying to fit the program into an already busy life. (The meetings can always be rescheduled if a participant has a conflict on a particular week.)

Sign a Contract

To formalize the commitment between partners, all program participants kick off their year together by signing a contractual agreement. We encourage you to send a signed copy to us for an added accountability boost. Putting your signature to this agreement is a powerful and meaningful way to increase follow-through on the program over the course of a year. Contracts carry a great deal of symbolic meaning and can support completing the commitment to something that you really want to do, even when it gets challenging.

Component #6: Compassionate & Nonjudgmental Approach

The "No-Judgment" [approach] really took off that pressure of feeling like you had to be perfect. And I think that's huge because, although you might think "oh well, if it was that kind of environment, wouldn't you do more . . . ?" But life happens, and you have goals and you have things that you want to do, but things don't always go as planned. So, the fact that you get to go to someone you know is loving you through this, who is not judging you, if you didn't do all the three things that you said you were going to do, it really makes you want to do it more. And so I look forward to my meetings every week, because I know that I'm not going to be judged.

— Tatiana, 43, CoJourn participant paired with a colleague

CoJourn is designed to be experienced as fun, light and positive, and should ideally help create a relaxed, easeful process of empowerment and change. This often requires CoJourn partners to continuously remind each other that this program is not another way to feel badly about themselves.

We believe a relaxed, loving, self-compassionate approach makes the program feel more possible to sustain over time (and much more fun!).

Research shows: self-criticism undermines our motivation. In contrast, engaging in self-compassion is very strongly related to:

- Mental well-being
- Less depression, anxiety, stress, perfectionism
- Positive states like happiness and life satisfaction
- Greater motivation, taking greater self-responsibility, making healthier lifestyle choices
- A greater connection with others – better interpersonal relationships. [3]

(see Kristin Neff - self-compassion.org)

Because many of us are harder on ourselves than on even our worst enemies, holding a spirit of self-compassion can be very difficult for most people. This is where your CoJourn Partner comes in!

- During check-ins, be sure to honor a spirit of non-judgment, and remind your partner of self-compassion and interrupt any patterns of self-loathing, criticism, and harshness with oneself.
- If your partner did not complete one (or all!) of their set goals, remind them that this is okay, and is to be expected when working toward sustained change.
- If your partner did not succeed in a goal, it may be that it was a bit beyond the place where they are. They might need more support or a different intention, more of a baby step to where they would like to go.

Component #7: Spirit of Celebration

What CoJourn has brought me is a real sense of accomplishment in my personal life, and a great reminder for me to think about what an accomplishment / intention actually is. Before I started, I never would have given myself credit for reading a book. Or cleaning out a bookshelf (I got 100+ books cleaned out Sunday!) . . . but now I am allowing myself to be successful. What a great gift! Now I celebrate the small successes.

– Susan, 45, paired with a friend

Holding a spirit of celebration is about the way you treat yourself when you do succeed in completing one of your goals. Keeping this in mind will help you and your partner maintain a positive tone throughout the program and will allow you to stay motivated and keep moving along your path.

Research shows: taking time to celebrate small achievements changes your physiology and releases endorphins that increase well-being. It also increases feelings of pride and builds confidence, both of which make us want to try even harder.[4]

Acknowledging and celebrating small wins can create a "success mindset," which can boost morale and help keep you going during times of challenge. According to research on our negativity biases, negative experiences tend to have a greater impact on us than positive ones. To account for this, we need to actively internalize positive experiences by giving at least five times more attention to what we did well rather than focusing on what we did wrong.[5]

And since it can be easier to celebrate others rather than ourselves, CoJourn partners can remind one another to maintain this celebratory orientation. This practice of celebration can help cultivate a habit of gratitude, which has many benefits for mental and physical health.

Component #8: Singular Focus on One Area of Change

I would say that the biggest thing that doing CoJourn for the whole year did for me was just being able to keep in mind the bigger picture while still (being) able to accomplish the smaller, more menial, week-to-week tasks that just need to get done in order to be a successful person.
— Tom, 34, CoJourn participant, paired with a friend

CoJourn was designed to go against some of our inclinations to want to do everything, change everything right away, by centering a singular focus on one area of change.

In almost all cases, taking on too many areas of change simultaneously can be overwhelming, unfocused, and a recipe for disappointment.

Research shows: multitasking is not particularly effective and negatively impacts performance, and can be associated with negative outcomes such as depression and social anxiety.[6]

By narrowing the focus of CoJourn to a single broad area of your life (your "Guiding Theme") and creating weekly progress goals, you will have the opportunity to receive the benefit of consistency and real sustained movement in one focused area of your life.

Even when it feels like no progress is being made from the day-to-day perspective, revisiting your Guiding Theme and creating Weekly Milestones will add up over the year to create observable change.

Core Components Review and Reflection Questions

Eight Core Components:

1. Peer Support
2. Confidentiality
3. Active Listening
4. Accountability
5. Commitment
6. Compassionate/Nonjudgmental Approach
7. Spirit of Celebration
8. Singular Focus on one area of Change

After you read through the Eight Core Components, answer these questions, and discuss with your partner:

1. Which of the Eight Core Components come most easily to you, or do you already practice in your everyday life?

   _____
   _____

2. What feels exciting to you about these Core Components?

   _____
   _____

3. Which of the Core Components do you still have questions about?

   _____
   _____

4. What fears or concerns do you have connected to enacting (and sustaining) these Core Components?

   _____
   _____

5. Which of the Eight Core Components do you think will be most difficult for you to sustain?

   _____
   _____

   a. Why do you feel they would be difficult for you?

      _____

   b. What can you do to support yourself with this component?

      _____

   c. What can your CoJourn partner do to support you with this component?

      _____

6. Any other thoughts or reactions that would be helpful to share with your partner?

   _____
   _____

STEP 3

Commit—Create and Sign the CoJourn Contract

As you begin your CoJourn experience, it is important to set expectations and create an agreement with your partner. We recommend creating a written contract together that includes the following components:

Length of Program – establish whether you want to do the program from 3 months, 6 months, or a year (you can always extend the program if you both decide to!) We recommend a minimum of 3 months, and a maximum of a year. Most organizational programs are 3 months in length.

Check-In Meeting Time – look at your calendar with your partner, and determine a time block that will work for you both to schedule a 30-minute meeting every week. Then, plan your life around it, so you can be available as often as possible, and keep rescheduling to a minimum.

Check-In Length – It can be helpful to talk ahead of time about a target meeting length. We recommend making it a minimum of 20 minutes, and a maximum of 45 minutes to support enough time for some depth, while remaining short enough for sustainability.

Mode of Communication – Talk with your partner about how you would like to meet. Remember, the value of CoJourn hinges on actually speaking with your partner (rather than emailing or texting). If you live close to your partner, face-to-face meetings can be a satisfying and meaningful way to talk. After face-to-face, we recommend video check-ins as a decent second option, but this isn't always realistic for everyone. Talking on the phone is another viable option and the most flexible choice.

Tone of the Check-in – Have a conversation about your preference for tone—playful, light and fun, or more serious and formal. This will be helpful to check in about throughout the process. Striking a balance is important.

Other Agreements to Include – You may want to talk about the level of confidentiality you would like for the program (is the fact that you are doing CoJourn together something you would like to keep between the two of you?). You also may want to touch base about altering the guidelines of CoJourn to make it work best for you and your partner. Finally, we encourage you to put your personality and a bit of flair into the contract, whatever would make it feel like it is *yours*.

Example Contract

Here is an example Contract that we created that you can draw from (or copy.)

NOTE: We realize that the contract below sounds formal and not quite in line with the typical tone of CoJourn. We both like the formality—it's a bit tongue-in-cheek, and we feel it signifies the importance of the elements of the program and the importance of following through on our own life and dreams. That said, feel free to adapt this language in any way that feels good to you!

CoJourn Contract

_____, known as "First Party," agrees to enter into this contract with _____, known as "Second Party," for collaboration on CoJourn beginning on _____ and terminating on _____.

This agreement is based on the following provisions:

1. The two parties agree to a weekly in-person, video, or phone check-in to review Weekly Milestones. Both parties will share successes and struggles with said goals. Then, each party will set new Weekly Milestones.
2. This check-in will happen no matter what, and both parties will take equal responsibility for making contact. If one party is excessively cranky, they may be honest and keep contact brief, but they still must have the conversation. Both parties must make a concerted effort to engage in complete honesty with one another and simultaneously be kind to one another.
3. Both parties agree to be intentional about keeping check-ins to a maximum of 30–45 minutes.
4. Confidentiality will be maintained for anything shared by one's CoJourn partner in the context of this program. Exceptions may be made in the case of therapeutic relationships or with expressed permission of both parties. Parties may discuss the program with each other at additional times, but each party always has permission to decline speaking about it outside of agreed-upon weekly check-in times.

5. Weekly check-ins will be held every _____ [Enter Day of the Week] at _____ [Enter Time] (or another set weekly time as schedules change). Both parties must do everything they can to keep this appointment. However, if one party is unavailable, it is their responsibility to make alternative arrangements for a check-in within a 24-hour window.
6. Both parties agree to do their best to keep this program easeful and fun and to NOT use it as another excuse to feel badly about themselves.

Furthermore, the First Party agrees:

To listen carefully to the Second Party, paraphrase, and enter expressed notes and milestones into the Field Notes document within 24 hours of check-in. Also, to do everything within her / his / their power to be fully present and encouraging of the other party throughout the entire process, keeping their partner's best interests in mind (in addition to her / his / their own).

and the Second Party agrees:

To listen carefully to the First Party, paraphrase, and enter expressed notes and milestones into the Field Notes document within 24 hours of check-in. Also, to do everything within her / his / their power to be fully present and encouraging of the other party throughout the entire process, keeping their partner's best interests in mind (in addition to her / his / their own).

This agreement is subject to the laws and regulations of _____(country, city, state).

Signed:

_____

[First Party Name]

_____

[Second Party Name]

_____

[First Party Signature]

_____

[Second Party Signature]

_____

[Date]

_____

[Date]

STEP 4

Develop a Guiding Theme

Overview – Goals vs Intentions

Now that you have decided to commit to CoJourn with a partner, it's time to begin the exciting process of choosing which area of your life to focus on. For some people, this might be very clear from the start, for others, it might take a little more reflection. Below is some information and examples that might help you as you make this decision.

How Do We Distinguish Between Goals and Intentions?

Intention: *How you want to be*. An intention is a way of being. It's not something that can be counted or precisely measured, rather it's something you aim for. In contrast to a specific goal, an intention is process-oriented. It's a guide or reminder for how you want to live and behave (i.e., your Guiding Theme for CoJourn—the path you commit to).

Goal: *What you want to do*. A goal is an aim with a concrete, specific, and measurable outcome and result. Goals are action-oriented (as opposed to process-oriented) and involve finishing something in a real measurable sense (i.e., your weekly goals that keep you on your path).

The Guiding Theme

Your Guiding Theme is an *intention* related to one area of your life that you would like to pay consistent, sustained attention to (with support) over the course of the program.

Since the Guiding Theme is an intention rather than a specific goal, it should be:

- Broad,
- Non-measurable,
- Flexible enough to be relevant for the duration of the program,
- Generative and healthy for you and your life.

The Guiding Theme is not a specific destination but the path you want to follow—a direction toward which you consistently move.

For example, a *goal* of running a marathon could be accomplished within a few months, whereas the *intention* (Guiding Theme) to "prioritize living in a more healthy and active manner" can take many forms throughout the program, and have many sub-goals and intentions associated with it that can shift with a changing life. One of those larger sub-goals might be to run a marathon.

Tips for the Guiding Theme

TIP #1: Remember that when deciding on a Guiding Theme there is no "one size fits all" model.

Choosing a Guiding Theme is personal and individualized because we all have different patterns, strengths, and areas of struggle. It is important that the wording of your Guiding Theme resonates for you. Even if it isn't clear to your partner or others, as long as it speaks to you it is probably the right intention for you.

For one person, being more proactive or going "full throttle" in their life could be the perfect Guiding Theme. For another person, who might have a tendency to do too much and overextend themselves, this same intention could be unhealthy. Making a Guiding Theme to slow down and let themselves off the hook might be a more appropriate intention.

TIP #2: Try to opt for an "Enlivening" Guiding Theme.

An enlivening Guiding Theme feels like a gift to yourself, something just for you. It's something that speaks to what you really want out of life. It may feel simultaneously thrilling and scary, but also joyful. It brings you energy and lights you up.

An enlivening Guiding Theme is in contrast to one that comes from your "inner critic," or from a spirit of self-deprecation, self-critique, or a sense of what other people think you should be doing with your life.

TIP #3: Ask yourself some of these helpful questions when thinking about a Guiding Theme.

- What would make the biggest difference in my life right now?
- As I name this intention, does it feel light, or heavy?
- Is this something I feel excited to pursue, or does it feel like drudgery?
- Is it sustainable over the course of the program?
- Is it broad enough to allow for a number of different kinds of weekly goals and intentions?

TIP #4: Check in with your partner—is your Guiding Theme something they can fully support you with?

Certain topics may be triggering and painful for some people, based on their own lived experiences. For example, if your partner has a history of struggling with an eating disorder, it may be a challenge for them to support you with a Guiding Theme connected to weight loss or fitness.

TIP #5: Take time to find the right Guiding Theme and wording that resonates with you.

It may take a few weeks to narrow down what you want your Guiding Theme to be. That is okay—we encourage you to take the time to find an intention that feels right for you. Ask for help from your CoJourn partner in talking through the details and purpose of the intention. If writing your Guiding Theme as a statement feels hard, consider writing it as a question (How can I be the healthiest, strongest version of myself?). Or, some participants have had a positive experience using a metaphor (i.e., The Year of The Butterfly).

Guiding Theme Examples

Examples of Broad Categories to Consider:

- Eating / Drinking Healthfully
- Exercise and Fitness
- Thoughtful Money Habits
- Stress-Relief / Rest / Balance
- Social Activism
- Decluttering / Simplifying
- Spirituality
- Friendships
- Relationships at Work
- Presence / Mindfulness
- Mental Health / Self-Care
- Overcoming Self-Doubt
- Creativity
- Romantic Relationships
- Relationship with Self

Example Guiding Themes from Participants:

- Working on feelings of belonging
- Be more real, more present, more vulnerable
- Prioritizing creativity in my life
- Caring for my Environment (home, family, world)
- Prioritizing my own happiness
- Quieting Myself / Slowing Down
- Strengthening the "Four Pillars" (spiritual-mental-physical-emotional)
- Feeling strong, fit, and comfortable in my body
- Set up my environment to support my success
- Follow Through (both professional and emotional)
- Being proactive (socially, financially, professionally, creatively, etc.)
- Use my gifts and abilities out in the world (Being Big)
- Overcoming Fear – going "Full Throttle"
- Be more loyal to dreams than to fears

Guiding Theme Brainstorming Worksheet

I. Free-Write

Set a timer for five minutes and then look at the following questions and write everything that comes to mind. Don't stop to think about what you're writing, and don't bother editing or censoring anything in any way. Keep your pen continuously moving and try to write as much as you can.

Main Questions

Imagine it is one year in the future. You're looking back over the past year and thinking WOW! That was the best year I've ever had. I am living in alignment with my truest purpose and values. I feel expanded, energized, and as if I'm living the life I truly want to be living.

- What happened this year to create these conditions?
- What does your life look like?
- What does it feel like?
- What have you accomplished?
- How do you spend your time?
- With whom do you spend your time?
- What changes have you made from where you were a year ago?

_____
_____
_____
_____
_____
_____
_____
_____
_____
_____
_____
_____
_____
_____

Supporting Questions

As you look at where you are right now in comparison to where you want to be in a year:

- What is an area of struggle where you could use some support and sustained attention?

  _____
  _____
  _____

- What is an area of strength that you would like to build on this year?

  _____
  _____
  _____

- What is one change you could make to be more in line with your values and vision of who you want to be in the world?

  _____
  _____
  _____

- What is something that would make your life better?

  _____
  _____
  _____

- What would move you forward and help you feel more like the best version of yourself?

  _____
  _____
  _____

2. Organize

Now take these notes and drawings and see if you can pull out coherent themes from the jumble. Do you see any patterns? Are there certain concerns that keep popping up? Try to organize these thoughts into some categories or, if any jump out, potential ideas or phrases for a Guiding Theme.

3. Prioritize

As you read through and prioritize your possible path, consider these questions:

- What would make the biggest difference in your life right now?
- As you name this theme, does it feel light and expansive? Why or why not?
- Is this something you feel excited to pursue, or does it feel like drudgery? Why?
- Is it broad, flexible enough, and sustainable to work on over the course of the program (typically 12 weeks or a year)?
- Does this intention feel like a "Hell, Yes!"?

4. Develop and Try it Out

Chat with your CoJourn partner to further flesh out your ideas, and work on developing wording that resonates for you. Test out your Guiding Theme for the first couple of weeks of the program, and adjust as needed.

If you are still having difficulty, it may help to try different approaches. You can look for an image that would help you, such as to "let my butterfly fly" or "chasing the sun." You may also like to use a more exploratory question. So instead of a command like "Be my most creative self" you might want to word it as "How can I take more creative risks?"

STEP 5

Create and Record Weekly Milestones

Weekly Milestones are the smaller, more manageable stepping stones that keep you on the path of your Guiding Theme. Weekly Milestones may take the form of a *goal*, or they may be a mini-*intention*. Both can be equally effective and powerful ways to keep you moving on your path.

Remember: *goals* are what you want to do whereas *intentions* are how you want to be. So when it comes to breaking down your larger aspirations, you can use both approaches each week to stay focused on your Guiding Theme.

Weekly Milestones fall into four categories:

I. Weekly SMART Goals

Specific – Is the goal you want to accomplish clear and distinct?
Measurable – Can you quantify your goal to be able to tell if you've accomplished it?
Achievable – Is your goal small enough and manageable to accomplish in one week?
Realistic – Is your goal possible to accomplish *this week* with everything you have going on?
Time-based – Is there a clear deadline or specific timeframe for the goal?

These can be personal challenges or little attainable goals that can serve as stepping stones towards the Guiding Theme.

Ex. for a Guiding Theme of "slowing down," a weekly goal might look like "Commit to 10 minutes of meditation every morning for a week."

2. Weekly Intentions

These smaller intentions or themes for the week are not concrete, measurable goals. Instead, they're areas to focus on or pay attention to that relate to your Guiding Theme.

Ex. for the same Guiding Theme of "slowing down," a weekly intention could be "Take a pause in between activities to ground myself and breathe."

3. 'Spirit Boosters'

These are intentions and goals you make to revitalize your spirit when you need to reset, rest, get into equilibrium, bounce back from a set-back, or have some fun. They may or may not be measurable, but rather set the tone for your week to give you a boost when things get stale or during times of struggle. These may not necessarily relate directly to your Guiding Theme.

Sample 'Spirit Boosters':

- Try to have a spirit of: [generosity / patience / service / inclusiveness]
- Treat this week like your last week on earth–connect with people, play, do something new
- Focus on the present, and try to notice when you're caught up in past/future
- Be extra gentle with yourself this week
- Do one pleasurable thing each day.

4. 'Path Maintenance' Goals

These are your practical life support goals. Often unrelated to the Guiding Theme, these can be really useful to clear some space in your life and unblock you so you can focus back on your Guiding Theme.

Sample 'Path Maintenance' Goals:

- Spend 2 hours on the weekend cleaning out your basement
- Find a new doctor this week
- Get all of your tax documents together to prepare for filing

- Make an appointment with the auto mechanic to see what that weird sound is
- Mow the lawn after work.

Sample Weekly Milestones

Guiding Theme: "Quieting Myself"

Sample Weekly Milestones:

- Commit to 10 minutes of meditation every morning
- Have at least one evening where you stay at home
- Clean up the big pile of papers in the corner of your room
- Make an effort to pause, take deep breaths and slow down when communicating with people at work.

Guiding Theme: "Building More Authentic Relationships"

Sample Weekly Milestones:

- Push yourself to have lunch with a friend and ask them questions about their life
- Write a letter to someone
- Opt away from virtual relationships / texting and choose more in-person contact with others
- Have that difficult conversation with a friend that you've been putting off.

Guiding Theme: "Prioritizing Creative Pursuits"

Sample Weekly Milestones:

- Buy yourself a new set of watercolors
- Set aside one evening to paint
- Invite a friend to attend an art gallery opening with you
- When moving through the week, try to take time to notice "art" around you (e.g., graffiti, a beautiful sunset, interesting architecture).

Guiding Theme: "Becoming More Proactive (career-finance-relationships)"

Sample Weekly Milestones:

- Create a budget this week
- Cook for yourself 3 times
- Make your own coffee to bring to work, rather than buying every day
- Schedule a meeting to talk with your boss about a raise
- Try out one internet dating app this week.

Recording Weekly Milestones

Example Use of the Field Notes Spreadsheet

You can download this spreadsheet at www.cojourn.org/field-notes to keep track of your Weekly Milestones. This process of recording milestones will allow you to reflect, learn, and adjust your approach along the way. And at the end of the program, you will have some interesting and useful data to learn about your patterns, successes, and failures.

If you do not care for spreadsheets, you can also keep track of goals using pen and paper, or in a shared word document. We do recommend though that you make sure that all milestones are all recorded in one place so you can go back and review your progress.

CoJourn
STAY THE PATH WITH "TOGETHER-HELP"

Week		FRANK		JERRY	
		Guiding Theme		Guiding Theme	
		Making the healthier choices (exercise, eating, drinking, sleeping)		Being more aware and present in the moment - enjoy the ride!	
Start	End	Weekly Milestones	Notes	Weekly Milestones	Notes
1/1/2020	1/7/20	1) Limit drinks to only the weekend this week 2) Find a healthy recipe to make food once this week 3) Try to get 8hrs of sleep 3 nights, make it a priority	Each week, Jerry enters the milestones Frank has set	1. Take 30sec to reflect on what you just finished doing before jumping to the next thing 2. Don't work through the lunch break a few times this week - take the time to just chat with friends and enjoy that 3. Plan some fun activities for after work - pickup basketball, or trivia night 4. Set aside 10min before the big presentation to just collect your thoughts and relax a bit	
1/8/20	1/14/20	1) At birthday party, just try to be aware of each beer you drink, noticing what each one tastes like and how it feels 2) Make a healthy breakfast Monday and Tues before work (oatmeal and fruit!) 3) Finally buy that gym membership 4) Call to make doctor's appt 1) To make exercise a little more social and fun, try out a few classes at the gym	J: Frank's been way more aware of his alcohol habits and how it makes him feel. Cut mostly out during the week and sounds like it's been making exercising a lot easier to do. Plus finally signed up for a gym to hopefully give him a way to exercise easily after work even if it's bad out. Jerry can also add notes to help Frank remember how the weeks have gone	1. Repeat the 30sec reflection from last week before jumping to the next part of the day 2. Try working without music the whole day and see if it helps feel like you're more with it 3. Take a break to walk around every hour and chat with people at work	

STEP 6

Meet Weekly with Your Partner

The Structure of the Weekly CoJourn Meeting

Below are the clear steps of how to structure your weekly meeting with your CoJourn partner. Note, the very first meeting will be slightly different since you will not yet have weekly milestones to report. During that first meeting, you will finalize your Guiding Theme, and create Milestones for the upcoming week.

Check-Ins (Week 1):

The first week's check-in will be slightly different from other weeks:

- ○ Take turns to finalize Guiding Themes.
- ○ Brainstorm broader goals and intentions related to the Guiding Theme.
- ○ Generate three to five milestones for the first week of the program.

Check-Ins (Weeks 2–52):

The CoJourn check-in structure involves taking turns to talk so that both partners can fully express and think through their milestones, while working out what they need without outside interruption. Using the structure helps keep weekly check-ins to a more consistent and sustainable length (ideally 30 minutes).

Step 1: Greetings and Start

- a. Say hello, perhaps catch up a bit, and confirm the amount of time you have for the check-in this week (we recommend aiming for 30 minutes a week).
- b. Decide who will go first to check-in (we find it helpful to alternate the order weekly).

Step 2: Last Week's Recap

- The speaker: shares how they did on last week's goals. What went well or what obstacles got in the way of Weekly Milestones?
- The listener:
  - supplies external accountability
  - gives support
  - actively listens
  - reminds the speaker of the compassionate, nonjudgmental approach
  - provides guidance and advice (when requested).

Step 3: Discuss Upcoming Week

- The speaker:
  - reminds themselves of the context of what is coming up this week
  - restates their Guiding Theme
  - creates three to five mini goals or intentions that will move them on the path they set for themselves.
- The listener:
  - paraphrases and records their partner's goals for them
  - reads the goals back to check for accuracy.

Step 4: Record

- Both partners record each other's milestones into some sort of shared document (your Field Notes).

Step 5: Switch Roles

Step 6: Wrap Up and Closing

- Partners confirm the meeting time for the following week and close the CoJourn part of the call.

Note – we recommend doing "process" check-ins periodically throughout the experience to see how the program is feeling for both partners (see questions in the next section [Step 7]).

STEP 7

Work with Your Partner and Make Adjustments Along the Way

A key part of the CoJourn experience is to have conversations with your CoJourn partner to reflect together and talk about the process. Below are questions to support these conversations at the start, midpoint, and completion of your CoJourn experience. Feel free to add in extra process check-ins along the way if it feels needed or useful for you.

If you are having any difficulties with the experience or with your partner, we also encourage you to check out Chapter 8 in our book, *CoJourn: Harnessing the Power of Connection to Tune into Your Wisdom, Achieve Your Goals, and Create the Life You Want.* This chapter includes advice and ways to work with a number of different partner challenges.

Kicking-off and Setting Expectations

The best way to work through potential challenges and tangles with your CoJourn partner is to avoid getting into them in the first place. We encourage teams to have a process check-in before beginning CoJourn. This will allow you and your partner to get to know one another better and have a chance to talk about each other's individual needs, patterns, and challenges. It's helpful for both partners to clearly state their personal hopes for the program and their expectations from their partner. It can also be useful to clarify the level of confidentiality that each person would like with CoJourn (would they like the fact that they are doing the program at all to be confidential, or just the content of sessions, etc.).

We also advise checking in about your partner's feelings around additional support during the week: would you like to receive a text message from your partner on a day when you have something challenging going on or to encourage you on a particular goal? Or would receiving texts like "You've got this! I believe in you!" make your skin crawl and annoy you? It's good to be clear with one another about such things right from the get-go.

CoJourn Journey Kick-off Questions:

Below are a few questions to explore individually and then with your partner to aid you in setting expectations before you begin CoJourn:

1. What is your motivation for trying CoJourn?
2. If this program is successful, what will that look like for you?
3. What are your hopes for the end of the program?
4. What are your biggest worries and concerns connected to this program?
5. What are three things that would be helpful for your partner to know about you in order to best support your process?
6. What is your typical way of being when you're having a hard time? (I.e., do you disappear, and not call back, shut down, cry, etc). What do you need from your partner at these times?
7. How do you like to celebrate when you succeed at something? What do you need from your partner at these times?
8. What are your key areas of strength in relation to this program? (I.e., the structure, upholding the 8 Core Components, etc.)? What comes easily / naturally to you?
9. What are some areas for growth, or where do you anticipate that you may need additional support?
10. In your role as a supporter of your partner, what are 2–3 descriptors of your own interpersonal style that you think might be helpful to talk about?

Based on the "data" gathered, what are some of the emerging patterns / themes and variations that may impact your CoJourn relationship?

Mid-Journey Process Check-In

As you move through your CoJourn experience it can be helpful to revisit the expectations set at the beginning through semi-regular process check-ins with your partner. Setting aside time to have this conversation can support you to have the courage and space to bring up issues that, if resolved, would improve your experience. Even in the best working relationships, this scheduled time can ensure you're getting the most out of your experience together. Below are some questions to support this process.

Process Check-In Questions to Explore with your Partner:

1. How do you both feel about your experience with CoJourn so far?
2. How are you doing with the hopes and concerns that you expressed when you first began the program?
3. What are some things that you appreciate about our CoJourn partner—what's working?
4. What are some things that your partner could do to make the process even better?
5. How are you doing with upholding the Eight Core Components of CoJourn?
   - Active Listening
   - Peer Support
   - Confidentiality
   - Accountability
   - Commitment
   - A Nonjudgmental Approach
   - A Celebratory Spirit
   - Singular Focus on One Area for Change
6. How have you been doing with your weekly meetings?
   - Are they consistent?
   - Are they a good length?
   - Does the time work?
   - Do they feel fun?
7. What have you learned through the process so far?

End of CoJourn Celebration and Reflection

Congratulations! If you are working with this page, it most likely means that you have successfully completed your full CoJourn experience.

We encourage you to do something special to celebrate this occasion by planning an outing or a night out: go out to dinner together, go camping, go to an amusement park, go on a road trip, see some live music, go skydiving, get creative!

- If you don't live near each other, brainstorm something that would be fun for you both. Or plan to give a small gift to commemorate the year together.

In addition, your Field Notes (where you record your Weekly Milestones) contain a wealth of useful material. Looking through these carefully at the end of the year (alone and with your partner) can reveal a great deal of information about your growth and habitual patterns. This information is valuable for increasing self-awareness and thinking ahead to next year.

We encourage you to free-write your answers to the questions below, and then meet up with your CoJourn partner to talk through them together.

End of Journey Reflection Questions

- Review the notes from the year together and reflect:
  - What were some of your favorite stories from the year?
  - What were some of the most memorable challenges and successes?
  - What did you learn about yourself from the experience?
  - Reflect on your and your partner's Guiding Themes and how you saw progress in both.
- Take time to express appreciation for your CoJourn partner:
  - What were some things you learned from each other?
  - What were some changes you noticed in your partner?
  - How were you inspired or impressed by your partner?

STEP 8

Reflect and Celebrate

There is a great deal you may be able to learn about yourself throughout the process of CoJourn. We encourage you to be curious, experiment with new behaviors, and notice your cyclical patterns with the help of the "data" you collect in your Field Notes. Use the weekly check-in to reflect on what's working, and what you can adjust.

Also, take time to appreciate the relationship you develop with your partner. These types of relationships, where we get to show more of ourselves to another person, are becoming increasingly rare in our busy, disconnected society. And, research shows these close, connected relationships are the number one predictor of happiness and well-being in life.

FREQUENTLY ASKED QUESTIONS

When Is the Right Time to Get Started with CoJourn?

Many people like to start CoJourn around their birthday or a new year—it's one way to keep a New Year's resolution for a full year. Others participating in a 12 Week program may start at the beginning of a season. However, beginning CoJourn shouldn't be limited to any month or time of year. You can get started any time.

If you think you should wait to get started because you're too busy, we want to remind you that you'll always be busy. Start now!

You can find thirty minutes a week to prioritize you. And we promise you'll be glad you did. With that said, the program can be great to help with focus and balance during:

- Start of a new job
- Start of a school year
- During or after a move
- When you meet a new friend you want to connect with
- When you want to reconnect with an old friend or family member
- Any transition period.

What Would I Get Out of Participating in CoJourn?

Data from past CoJourn participants reveal numerous benefits related to follow-through on goals and building a closer relationship with someone else.

A few repeatedly mentioned benefits include:

- Sustained focus and follow-through on something you want in your life
- The benefit of slowing down and taking time for weekly reflection

- A closer relationship with another person who knows about your life
- The gift of learning from the struggles and successes of your partner

What Is CoJourn's Mission?

The program's mission is to:

1. Counter the increased disconnection we've experienced in our fast-paced, technology-driven society, and
2. Provide a tool accessible to all to help with follow-through on a single life intention for one year.

I Hate the Phone! Can We Just Do Our Check-Ins via Text or Email?

When we created CoJourn, we were immersed in recent research on technology's impact on human connection. We were reading studies that showed in-person contact and talking on the phone were in decline, leading to many public health concerns. We were also reading about the benefits of real-time communication, both in terms of happiness and physical well-being. For this reason, we created CoJourn as a program to provide a structure for people to talk to each other and tap into the magic that can happen when we are deeply listened to and supported by another human. Because of this, we strongly discourage doing this program via email or text—we don't believe it will work. However, a quick written check-in may be needed once in a while throughout your process if one person is traveling, etc. This is fine, though we encourage you to make it the exception rather than the rule.

What Is the Weekly Time Commitment?

We recommend setting aside a full thirty minutes a week for the CoJourn check-in. Most people find this to be a suitable amount of time to have an in-depth talk with someone while still keeping the program sustainable even during the busiest times.

Can I Keep the Same Milestones Every Week or Should I Change Them?

This is completely up to you! Some people like to work toward the same milestones for a number of weeks in a row, while others may find that milestones get stale quickly and want to change things up. It can also be helpful to cycle milestones in and out depending on what your needs are. CoJourn is for you, so test it out and see what's the most helpful.

I Am Worried About My Partner, What Should I Do?

If you feel concerned that your partner is experiencing a mental health crisis and is in danger of hurting themselves or others, it is important to break confidentiality and get in touch with some outside help. If you are doing the program on your own, you could express your concern to another member of their family or one of their friends without sharing details of their CoJourn check-in. If you are part of an organizational program, you can contact the liaison within the organization who is coordinating CoJourn, or a CoJourn coach within the organization. There are also national hotlines you can call for support and advice from professionals. In the U.S. you can contact the National Suicide Prevention Lifeline at 1-800-273-8255, the National Alliance of Mental Illness hotline at 1-800-950-6264 or helpline@nami.org or you can text the Crisis Text Line by texting "HOME" to 741741.

ENDNOTES

1   Dominican University of California," Study Backs up Strategies for Achieving Goals," 2013, http://www.goalband.co.uk/uploads/1/0/6/5/10653372/strategies_for_achieving_goals_gail_matthews_dominican_university_of_california.pdf; Nancy Anderson, "5 Ways To Make Your New Years Resolutions Stick," *Forbes*, January 03, 2013, http://www.forbes.com/sites/financialfinesse/2013/01/03/5-ways-to-make-your-new-years-resolutions-stick/#2fe8b0736c57;

2   For a review of the literature on accountability refer to Tom Tyler, "The psychology of legitimacy: A relational perspective on voluntary deference to authorities," *Personality and Social Psychological Review,* 1, (1997): 323-345; J.S. Lerner and P.E. Tetlock, "Accounting for the Effects of Accountability," *Psychological Bulletin,* 125, no. 2 (1997):255-275.

3   Kristin Neff, *Self-compassion: The Proven Power of Being Kind to Yourself* (New York: Harper Collins, 2011).

4   Ximena Vengeochear, "Here's why you should throw yourself a party the next time you reach a goal," *The Washington Post,* February 24, 2015, https://www.washingtonpost.com/news/inspired-life/wp/2015/02/24/want-to-keep-those-resolutions-then-learn-to-celebrate-your-wins/; Polly Campbell, "Why You Should Celebrate Everything, *Psychology Today,* Dec 2, 2015, https://www.psychologytoday.com/us/blog/imperfect-spirituality/201512/why-you-should-celebrate-everything.

5   Roy F. Baumeister et al., "Bad is Strong Than Good," *Review of General Psychology, 5,* no. 4 (2001): 323-370, DOI: 10.1037//1089-2680.5.4.323; Jason Kim, "3 Steps to Worry Less and Overcome Your Negativity Bias," *Positive Psychology,* July 16, 2019, https://positivepsychologyprogram.com/3-steps-negativity-bias/.

6   Sandra Chapman, "Why Single-Tasking Makes You Smarter," *Forbes*, May 08, 2013, http://www.forbes.com/sites/nextavenue/2013/05/08/why-single-tasking-makes-you-smarter/#31096e631b5c; Amy Dalton and Stephen A. Spiller, "Too Much of a Good Thing: The Benefits of Implementation Intentions Depend on the Number of Goals," *PsycEXTRA Dataset*, 2012. doi:10.1037/e665532012-001; Mark W. Becker et al., "Media Multitasking Is Associated with Symptoms of Depression and Social Anxiety," *Cyberpsychology, Behavior, and Social Networking* 16, no. 2 (2013): 132-135.

A NOTE FROM THE FOUNDERS

We hope you have a fun, connected, and transformative experience with CoJourn!

If you take anything from this experience, we would like for you to enjoy the journey, remembering to celebrate all of your successes along the way. Just the fact that you are embarking on a program like this is a cause to celebrate! So be sure to pat yourself on the back. Frequently.

In addition to making movement on all of your goals, we hope you develop a relationship where you can show more of your extraordinary self to another person, connect through imperfections, heartaches and disappointments AND revel in moments of courage, meaning, and the small successes that add up over time.

And if you haven't already, we encourage you to check out the full book *CoJourn: Harnessing the Power of Connection to Tune Into Your Wisdom, Achieve Your Goals, and Create the Life You Want* for more detailed information about the program, the research supporting it, and personal stories from us and many of the participants over the years.

Please do not hesitate to get in touch if we can be a resource to you along the way!

With love and gratitude,
Molly & Karl
Co-Founders of CoJourn

ABOUT THE AUTHORS

MOLLY KEEHN, ED.D. currently teaches courses at the undergraduate and graduate level and facilitates diversity, equity, and inclusion trainings in the academic, non-profit, and corporate sectors. She is also a writing coach, wine tasting associate, accordion player, triathlete, and eternal optimist. Molly lives in western Massachusetts with her pugs, Wilbur Noodles and Poppy Dumpling.

KARL HENRICKSEN has been a full-time professional musician, engineer and, more recently, audio technician and videographer. He performs as a solo singer and guitarist as well as occasionally with the family band, DH and the Gentleman (along with Molly, on accordion). Karl is an aspiring inventor and rides a hell of a skateboard, plays soccer, surfs, and bikes. He lives in Charleston, South Carolina, with his wife, Clarissa, and his three cats, Ravioli, Lasagna, and Yogna.

Connect with Us:
www.cojourn.org
Instagram: @cojourninternational
Facebook: @cojourn

www.ingramcontent.com/pod-product-compliance
Lightning Source LLC
Chambersburg PA
CBHW080602030426
42336CB00019B/3305